MAIDSTONE
BOROUGH BUSES
1974–1992

ERIC BALDOCK

AMBERLEY

Acknowledgements

All the photographs in this book are my own and are selected to show all the types owned (in their various liveries) and the majority of the hired buses. They have also been chosen to show buses in many town centre locations, the traditional terminals, post-1981 rural routes, suburban and central London. Coaches are shown in locations as far apart as Portsmouth, Burnley and northern France.

The captions and the fleet summary draw, with thanks, on the publications of the M&D and East Kent Bus Club. I would like to thank the following members of the club who have checked my text and helped make this book possible: Derek Jones, Norman Kemp, Nicholas King and Richard Lewis.

Front Cover: The traditional order at the High Street (Queen's Monument) stop in May 1977. Leyland Titan PD2A 24 (24 YKO) of 1963 was on morning peak standby duty for possible delays – it was the first day of road works for construction of the second bridge over the River Medway.

Back cover: Last of the batch of Volvo Citybuses for London Transport service 188, 914 (F114 TML) was picking up at St Pancras Church, the first stop south of Euston, on 4 September 1990.

Frontispiece: A feature of Maidstone Borough's buses was the number of different liveries carried. Vehicles of the same batch would have variations in livery and repaints of the same vehicle were common, especially on those buses that passed from the Maidstone Borough fleet to the Boro'line Maidstone fleet.

One example of this was 332 (CKN332Y) that was in the fleet from 1982 to 1988, and carried four liveries during this time. It was a short Bedford with a 35-seat Lex Maxeta body and was unique in the fleet. It was an unregistered demonstrator in Bedford stock when it was purchased. It initially ran, as acquired, in this rather unattractive fawn livery, as photographed at Grafty Green in February 1983. In August 1983, it was repainted in the standard brown and cream bus livery. This view shows it working in January 1984 on the short-lived service 91 that ran between Aylesford and the new Hospital at Barming. At this time there was no right turn from the London Road to Hermitage Lane, so the service had to double run via the Coldharbour Lane roundabout, which can be seen behind. In October 1986, the cream areas were painted yellow, for the interim Boro'line livery, as shown in this snowy January 1987 view at the Hospital. In March 1988, the brown areas were repainted blue, to achieve the full Boro'line livery.

First published 2010

Amberley Publishing Plc
Cirencester Road, Chalford,
Stroud, Gloucestershire, GL6 8PE

www.amberley-books.com

Copyright © Eric Baldock, 2010

The right of Eric Baldock to be identified as the Author of this work has been asserted in accordance with the Copyrights, Designs and Patents Act 1988.

ISBN 978 1 4456 0140 3

British Library Cataloguing in Publication Data.

A catalogue record for this book is available from the British Library.

Typesetting and Origination by Amberley Publishing.
Printed in Great Britain.

Contents

Introduction

Maidstone Corporation Transport followed a traditional course, and like many other towns around the country it began by running trams in 1904 and then buses in 1924. The trams were replaced between 1928 and 1930 mainly by trolleybuses, which were themselves replaced by buses in 1967.

The livery had always been various shades of brown with white or cream relief, but in 1965 the first of the trolleybus replacement fleet was delivered in a bright light blue and cream livery. The entire fleet carried this livery by 1969.

The local government reorganisation of 1974 saw Maidstone Corporation become Maidstone Borough Council and gain control of the rural district councils to the south and east of the town. It is from this point that this book takes up the story. Services, with two short exceptions, had always been limited to within the town boundary. Rural and interurban routes had always been the province of Maidstone & District; however, the new authority soon sought to serve its entire area. A single new route was soon introduced, jointly with M&D, but it was not until a major service reorganisation in 1981 that this aim was achieved.

Vehicle policy was quickly changed and new and second-hand single-deckers arrived to replace double-deckers. The fleet went from 100 per cent double-deck in 1974 to all single-deck by 1979. For a while spare vehicles were hired to other operators. Routes in the town were restructured and coaching operations were introduced for the first time. Acquired vehicles were often placed into service without repaint and in 1979 (following the painting of a bus in tram-style livery for the 75th anniversary) bus livery reverted to brown and cream.

Bus deregulation in 1986 saw further changes and the new 'arms length' operation was styled as Boro'line Maidstone. As well as a new commercial network around Maidstone, tendered services elsewhere in Kent and in London were gained from 1988. This resulted in new depots in south east London and a massive increase in fleet size. On the vehicle front double-deckers returned, and large fleets were hired in to introduce these new services, as deliveries of new buses were often delayed.

By 1989 operations were losing money and Alan Price, who had been in charge since 1974, left the following year. Competition appeared on routes in Maidstone initially with Bygone Buses, but from December 1991 M&D registered a competing network in Maidstone. Boro'line promptly countered with some commercial workings in the Medway Towns.

Meanwhile, attempts were being made to sell the business and the London operations, with 57 vehicles passed to Kentish Bus in February 1992. About the same time the Maidstone operation, with 61 vehicles, was placed into receivership. Services continued, despite some vehicles being repossessed, until 29 May 1992. The owned fleet and depot were sold to M&D, who took over Boro'line's contracts, including some Park & Ride workings.

In preparation is the prequel *Maidstone Corporation Trams and Buses 1904–1974*. The author is looking for any suitable pre-1970 colour views and any previously unpublished pre-1950 views and a complimentary copy will be available for the owner of any pictures used. Please contact the author via the publisher.

Eric Baldock MCILT
Ditton,
June 2010

MAIDSTONE BOROUGH TRANSPORT 1974–1986

A very traditional fleet passed from Maidstone Corporation Transport to the new Maidstone Borough Council on 1 April 1974. The older part of the fleet consisted of 18 Leyland Titans, all with Massey bodywork. They worked the Oxford Road to Ringlestone trunk route, various peak and infrequent routes. In September 1975, No. 23 (23 YKO) had dropped its last passengers at the London Road, Allington Way terminus, after working the afternoon school bus.

The remainder of the fleet consisted of 28 Leyland Atlanteans, which were fitted for one-man-operation and worked most of the network. Twenty had Massey bodywork and dated from between 1965 and 1968; they had been purchased mainly to replace the trolleybuses. No. 44 (OKJ 844F) of 1968 had left Tovil for Hatherall Road, also in 1975. It is followed by a Reed's Foden taking paper from their mill at Tovil.

The final eight Atlanteans from 1971/2 replaced the oldest Titans. By this time Massey had been taken over by their Wigan neighbour, Northern Counties, who supplied the bodywork for these vehicles. No. 48 (AKE 148K) was working to Gatland Lane in this 1975 view in Westree Road, passing the now demolished college buildings.

A timetable change on 11 November 1974 included the diversion of the Loose service to operate via Armstrong Road. Massey bodied Atlantean No. 32 (EKP232C) had turned from Postley Road into Armstrong Road soon after the introduction of this new routing.

Since 1972, repaints of Atlanteans featured a simplified livery application, with the blue carried up to the window line and without the black lining. In May 1974, Atlantean 38 (JKE 338E) appeared in this livery and also became the first vehicle to carry the new fleetname. Its staggered application and cream lettering was unique, as shown by this August 1977 view at Barming, Bull Inn. The pub can be seen in the background and the bus is standing on the second bay introduced in March 1976, following the withdrawal of the bus turning facility at Barming, Fountain Inn.

In July 1974, a more radical new half-and-half livery appeared on Atlantean 35 (JKE 335E). This late afternoon view shows it having just made a u-turn at the Queen's Monument while working a Penenden Heath to Allington Way journey. This move was only possible with the much wider road at this time and ceased with the service changes in conjunction with the opening of the Stoneborough (now Chequers) Centre on 15 November 1976.

Another livery experiment took place in December 1975, when Massey bodied Atlantean 37 (JKE 337E) gained a black engine cover in an attempt to stop engine oil marking the Fiesta blue livery. It was deemed less attractive than a few oily streaks and lasted only five months.

Four more Atlanteans (all of the 1968 batch) gained the half and half livery as demonstrated by 43 (NKK 243F) heading for Loose, in a rather run down Lower Stone Street in July 1975. These buses were known as the 'Wall's Ice Cream' buses as Wall's used a very similar livery on their vehicles at the time.

As a portent of things to come, two single-deck Ford demonstrators appeared in service in 1974. The second of these, Plaxton bodied NTW 438M, was photographed at the Loose terminus in August 1974.

Despite (or perhaps because of) the Ford demonstrators, four Willowbrook bodied 45-seat Bedford YRQs arrived in January 1975. Soon after entry into service, 57 (HKJ 257N) was picking up at the Fairmeadow stop while on service to Penenden Heath.

At a time when Maidstone buses were rarely seen outside the town, 58 (HKJ 258N) was recorded on a staff outing to London Zoo on 1 June 1975. In front of the bus is Len Leaver; he was the senior driver and also responsible for driver training and holiday cover for the mayor's chauffer.

Maidstone began its first Park & Ride service on 27 November 1975 from the lay-by in Week Street, to a parking area using an old section of the A20 by the Coldharbour Lane roundabout. Buses ran out via the London Road and back via the M20 and Sandling Road. In December 1975, 60 (JKN 60N), one of three more Willowbrook bodied Bedfords delivered in June 1975, basked in the afternoon sunshine awaiting returning passengers. Note the Park & Ride signs attached to the side of the bus, and on the bus stop.

Three more Bedfords taken into the fleet during the summer of 1975 were of the longer YRT models with 53-seat Duple Dominant bodywork. No. 62 (JKO 62N) was pictured at Allington Way in September of that year, still in pristine condition.

Revised schedules and new deliveries freed up older vehicles, which were not always withdrawn, and to gain revenue some buses were hired to other operators. Three Leyland Titans spent part of 1974 on hire to Alder Valley at Reading. Here No. 17 (517 RKR) had just emerged from the grim 1967 concrete bus station (now thankfully closed) having been let into the traffic queue by the driver of a Reading Borough Bristol RE.

The next hire was more substantial and lasted from October 1975 to September 1976 and involved six Titans at any time working for London Country at Dartford. They were suffering a major vehicle shortage and this period also featured Eastbourne AEC Regents at Swanley and Royal Blue Bristol coaches at Dunton Green. The Titans were usually employed on local service 499. In this view, 23 (23 YKO) was climbing the hill past Dartford Station, towards Joyce Green Hospital in December 1975. I recall sitting in my train home one evening and hearing a passing Leyland engine, in place of the normal AEC sounds. I found out a few days later about this hire and I knew exactly what I had heard!

The same day saw No. 17 (517 RKR) parked outside the depot at Dartford, in the company of an AEC Swift, in London Country green and an AEC Routemaster, in National green. Newer Titans 16 to 26 were technically PD2A models with the fibreglass radiator grill; older examples were PD2s and had metal grilles.

In January 1976, No. 14 (414 GKT) displays its metal grill and is at work on 499, in company with a London Country Bristol LH. Its days were numbered; it was hit in the rear by a London Country bus in March 1976 and withdrawn.

In March 1976, I organised an enthusiasts' tour of Maidstone for the M&D and East Kent Bus Club. My pictures taken on this day give a snapshot of operations at this time. It began with a depot visit and Atlantean 51 was taken through the bus wash for us.

Various broken Titans were found dumped outside the depot, most having succumbed to the rigours of operation in Dartford. The line was led by the recently withdrawn 14, with its rear end stoved in, but mechanically fit and able to donate its running gear to others.

Star of the tour was the oldest surviving Titan 12 (412 DKM). It was driven by Len Leaver and was posed at the departure stop at Tovil, Rose Inn, with a rare blind display. The shelter behind included a lockable toilet for staff use only; one end of each traditional route had such a facility. The paper mill building has long since been replaced by housing.

Meanwhile, Leyland Atlantean 29 (EKP 229C) had arrived on service and it was forced to wait on the arrival stop until No. 12 departed. Again, the paper mill has been replaced by housing.

No. 12 posed at the Barming, Banky Meadow terminus, an infrequent route via Queen's Road and at this stage still worked by Titans.

The frequent Ringlestone to Oxford Road service was also a Titan route and 22 (22 UKK) was captured turning from Hastings Road to Upper Road on a journey to Oxford Road.

Oxford Road is in the early post-war Shepway estate, to the south of the town and 25 (25 YKO) had just arrived at the terminus on the next journey from Ringlestone.

From 1974 Maidstone Borough took control of many of the villages south and east of the town and was keen to also serve this new area, deep in Maidstone & District territory. The first small step came with the introduction of a route from 6 October 1974 to serve the new estate at Madginford. This route was operated jointly with M&D and numbered 80. With a young Trevor Turner at the wheel, Atlantean 31 (EKP 231C) was standing at the Madginford terminus in Egremont Road, with No. 12 behind.

Another new housing area at this time was Senacre Wood. It was served by an infrequent service that terminated at the junction of Woolley Road and Reculver Walk. As you can see, the bus service started before many of the houses had been built. Atlantean 29 (EKP 229C) was at the terminus showing some replacement panels in the new livery application, giving a rather tatty appearance typical of the period.

The final view from this tour shows an infrequent extension of the Loose route, that had been introduced from 12 March 1973. Certain journeys were extended from the traditional Kings Arms terminus along Linton Road and then back north through Loose village. Northern Counties bodied Atlantean 49 (AKE 149K) was heading south on Linton Road.

Park & Ride operations continued into 1976, but the service was reduced to Tuesday (market day) and Saturday only in February and withdrawn entirely in April. During its operation three demonstrators were used, including LNM 318P a Tricentrol bodied Ford A 25-seater. Harris Carpets is now McDonalds.

In July 1976, two Ford Transits with 16-seat Strachans bodies were taken over from Denis Hire Cars, together with the Dial-a-Ride service from Maidstone East to the Loose and Coxheath areas. This operation had started in 1972 and sat between a taxi and a normal bus service. I remember one evening being in the Fisherman's Arms in Lower Stone Street, with the minibus parked outside and the driver getting his passengers from the bar! They ran initially in the orange and white livery used by Denis Hire Cars, with new fleetnames, as shown by the August 1976 shot at the Maidstone East terminus.

By February 1977, HOR 334L had been painted all blue, as recorded here at the Museum Street layover point. The outline borough crest on the driver's door was only ever carried by these two Transits and Atlantean 45.

Their final Fiesta blue and cream livery completed the Wall's Ice Cream look. By this stage the operation was much reduced and converted to a fixed route bus service. In August 1980, HOR 334L was being used as a service van, making a delivery to the Maidstone Borough Planning Office in Bedford Place.

Another demonstrator appeared in 1976 in the form of a South Yorkshire PTE Volvo Ailsa, with Irish built Van Hool-McArdle bodywork. It was registered LWB 405P and, with Len Leaver trying it out, it was photographed at the Gatland Lane terminus in November 1976.

Seven new Bedfords, of three different types, were taken into the fleet during 1976. Fleet numbers again reverted to 1 and the first coaches were taken into the fleet, to develop private hire work. No. 2 (NKE 302P), with 51-seat Duple Dominant Express bodywork, was running up the High Street in May 1976.

No. 3 (NKE 303P) was a 45-seat Duple Dominant bus, seen here emerging from Poplar Grove into the London Road on a morning peak journey from Palace Wood in February 1978, before traffic lights were installed at this junction.

The remaining four vehicles were 53-seat Duple Dominant buses, as exemplified by 7 (NKE 307P) seen in January 1977, running along the Tonbridge Road in appalling conditions. I suspect that today, with this much snow, nothing would be running!

Highlight of 1976 was the unexpected and unprecedented purchase of fourteen Leyland Leopards with Duple Dominant Express bodywork from Nottingham City Transport. They were only a year old and surplus from an experimental Park & Ride service. They were in lilac and maroon livery and all entered service in Maidstone in these colours. Four vehicles, including 16 (HNU 126N), were 51-seaters, mainly for coach use. It was photographed in Sudbury, Suffolk on an M&D and East Kent Bus Club trip in April 1977.

Six vehicles retained coach seats, but with enlarged luggage pens for bus work and seating capacity reduced to 49. No. 17 (HNU 117N) was one in this format and was pictured in the Broadway, passing Maidstone's War Memorial in March 1978.

Four vehicles were converted to buses, with 53 bus seats and 18 standing, to displace double-deckers from the busier workings. One of this type was 28 (JCH 398N), seen in Lower Stone Street working to Loose in January 1978.

15 November 1976 saw the opening of the bus road through Stoneborough (now Chequers) Centre and some routes were diverted this way. Northern Counties bodied Atlantean 53 (EKR 153L) was running through the bus road and had emerged into the sun at the southern end in February 1977. By this stage the newer (and more valuable) Atlanteans were being sold, so there was only a few months when these vehicles worked through here. Note the 'via Wrens Cross' on the destination blind, a name that now seems to have dropped out of use. How many Maidstonians today know what location is called Wrens Cross?

From February to November 1977 further buses were hired to London Country; this time it was Massey bodied Atlanteans at Chelsham depot. They generally worked service 403, as shown by 30 (EKP 230C) working at West Croydon Bus Station in May 1977.

At the other end of the route, at Warlingham Park Hospital, in June 1977 was half and half liveried 35 (JKE 335E).

This September 1977 view shows 27 (EKP 227C) parked up in the yard at Chelsham Depot, in the company of HLX 421, one of only five RTs to gain National green livery and a Routemaster coach in London Country green.

1976 saw a number of vehicles attend at Epsom for Derby Day. Double-deckers, especially open-toppers, are favoured as they serve as grandstands near to the finish line. Here No. 17 had just parked towards the finishing line. It lacked a destination blind, being between visits to Dartford. Even assuming all vehicles were fit, the number of buses here, plus those required for service in Maidstone and hire at Dartford, exceeded the total fleet!

The following year saw Atlanteans used and 39 (JKE 339E) was suitably decorated for the Queen's Silver Jubilee, which was to be celebrated a few days later. It had just come under the racetrack at Epsom, before parking in the centre of the course.

Just one new vehicle entered stock in 1977, 11 (SKN 491R), a long Bedford with 53-seat Willowbrook body. This vehicle was reputed to have a particularly difficult gearbox, and was said to have been partially responsible for the decision to order automatic gearboxes on subsequent deliveries. It was certainly rarely used outside peak times; I recall in 1980 looking at a wall chart in the depot showing vehicle mileages and this vehicle had about half that of the rest of the fleet. My May 1977 photograph shows it at the Cannon stop on a morning peak service to Park Wood.

Towards the end of Atlantean operation 45 (OKM 145G), in 'Wall's' livery and with the outline crest, picked up at Maidstone East station on a trip to Ringlestone in April 1978.

During 1978 double-deck operation became increasingly rare and scheduled operation ended in November 1978. The last one remaining in service was Titan 26 (26 YKO), which would often cover the Aylesford School contract morning and afternoon, followed by some evening peak trips on Banky Meadow to Vinters Park. This September 1978 view shows it on such a working just coming off London Road into Rocky Hill. It was the only Titan to carry the new fleetname. This operation came to an end in March 1979, when 26's engine expired.

1978 deliveries were twelve more Bedfords, all automatics and with Duple Dominant bodywork and eleven were long 61-seaters to replace double-deckers. In early November 1978, 67 (WKE 67S) was treading its way through the road works on Maidstone Bridge, associated with the building of the new bridge. In the background can been seen the remains of the Courage brewery and the Seven Greys pub.

The opening of the new St. Peter's Bridge and associated Town Centre Traffic Management Scheme resulted in a major timetable change, together with the general introduction of route numbers, from Sunday 12 November 1978. The new bridge was not opened until lunchtime (after the Remembrance Day diversions) and so for that morning only, buses with route numbers ran eastbound over the old bridge, as shown by Lilac Leopard 24 (HNU 124N).

The same morning saw Bedford 76 (AKK 176T), new only the previous month, work a westbound trip over the old bridge with cars still going the other way. To obtain 61 seats, these buses had 3+2 seating, making them especially cramped – they did, however, have wider four-leaf doors, following complaints that the two-leaf ones on earlier batches were too narrow and did not give access to firm handrails.

The changing of route numbers soon provoked objections from the drivers and their use was blacked, to use the term of the time. As a temporary bodge the Bedford buses gained route numbers on their destination displays, but as each destination had all the route numbers that went to that location, they were of little use. 62 (JKO 62N) was showing this futile arrangement in Mill Street in December 1978.

The agreed solution was to turn the blind boxes around so that the route number was on the offside, so both these and the destination could be changed without the driver leaving the cab. 70 (WKM 70S), the only short Bedford of the 1978 deliveries, was recorded with offside route number at the Cannon in March 1980.

This did not happen to some of the Bedfords, like 55 (HKJ 255N) seen here at the Cannon in May 1979, with nearside numbers in use (88 telling us this London Road service had come from Hatherall Road) and also numbers still on the destination blind.

Other changes to services from November 1978 included the extension of the Tovil service to become a circular route to serve new housing at Tovil Green. In February 1979, Leopard HNU 122N had reached the top of Burial Ground Road, having just passed my 1964 Hillman Minx.

In the town centre the flow on Gabriel's Hill was reversed – another view of 62 (JKO 62N) shows it emerging from Gabriel's Hill into the High Street in February 1981. Note the incorrect spelling of the destination, carried by the early Bedfords from new.

On 1 July 1979, a rally took place in Maidstone to celebrate 75 years of operation since the first trams in 1904. It was held on the Maidstone Market site and included several vehicles from the fleet, including withdrawn Titan 26 that was towed from Armstrong Road. Among the visiting vehicles was an unregistered Bedford JJL, which was later to run for Maidstone Borough. Also exhibited was Leyland Leopard 14 (GRC 884N) that, in April 1979, was the first Lilac Leopard to gain fleet livery following accident damage. At the same time it was fitted with roof-mounted destination equipment and named 'Maidstone Monarch'.

Star of the show was Bedford 75 (AKK 175T) that was painted into a dark brown livery based on that carried by the trams. It featured exclusive advertising for its sponsor and a commemorative plaque under the windscreen. No. 75 was seen here at the river end of the High Street a few days later.

Another Lilac Leopard, 28 (JCH 398N), following an accident gained a roof-mounted destination display in September 1979. This time the damage was such that a full repaint was not needed and the modified vehicle was seen in Lower Stone Street in November 1979, heading for Loose.

Vehicle shortages at Maidstone & District resulted in a couple of Bedfords being hired by Maidstone depot during much of 1979. This December 1979 picture shows Willowbrook bodied 59 (JKN 59N) at the Fiveways junction in Tunbridge Wells, heading back towards Maidstone via Tonbridge on service 7.

After selling four Titans to Lancaster in 1975, two Seddon Pennine bodied Leyland Leopards now came the other way, bringing another livery into the fleet. First to arrive was STD 119L, in December 1979. Initially numbered 29, it became 229 in the February 1980 renumbering scheme, as shown by this February 1981 view in Palace Avenue.

Second of the pair, STD 121L, arrived in February 1980 and was allocated number 212 in the new system. Accident damage again resulted in a Duple style front end being fitted in November 1980, with the exception of a small blue panel between the headlights, the front end was painted white. In its revised form it was recorded in August 1981, turning from Mill Street into the High Street.

STD 119L also gained a new front in August 1981; this time it was not due to an accident, but purely for cosmetic and standardisation reasons. On a snowy day in January 1982, STD 119L shows its new front in Museum Street. Note the lack of blue panel and heavy-duty bumper, as carried by its sister.

The final delivery in Fiesta blue livery, in January 1980, was 333 (HKN 333V), a Reeve Burgess bodied Transit, obtained to replace one of the 'Dial-a-Ride' fleet. It was photographed in March 1980 in Mill Street, with the Carriage Museum in the background.

It was not until November 1980 that the second one of the pair arrived, by which time a darker shade of blue, very similar to Lancaster livery and known as Nile blue, had been adopted for coaches. 336 (MKP 336W) was recorded at Ringlestone terminus on a Sunday in July 1981. By this stage the Sunday services were at a nadir, with buses running Loose–town centre–Ringlestone–Penenden Heath–town centre–Loose. Note the typical metal shelter and bus stop sign.

Two more Bedford/Duple coaches, this time with Dominant II Express bodywork, entered service in February 1980. They were 177 (JKM 277V named Maidstone Maiden) and 178 (JKM 278V – Maidstone Minstrel). The latter was recorded in June 1980 at Maidstone Barracks for the local heats of the Bus Driver of the Year Competition, in the company of Maidstone & District's Leyland Atlantean 558LKP, which was specially painted in traditional livery.

The first vehicles to appear in Nile blue were in fact normal repaints of ex Nottingham Leyland Leopards from June 1980. HNU 124N was picking up at the Pudding Lane bus stop on a Ringlestone working in July 1980, soon after repaint.

In March 1980, Bedford WKE 67S was leaving Earl Street to join Fairmeadow on an evening peak short working to connect with trains at Maidstone East. Behind the Fremlin's Brewery site can be seen, although by this date brewing had ceased and it was used only as a distribution depot. Today the House of Fraser is on this corner of the Fremlin Walk shopping centre.

The first repaint to adopt the brown and cream bus livery, similar to the tram-derived livery on AKK 175T, was short Bedford WKM 70S. This appeared in December 1980, following accident repairs during which it gained a heavy-duty front bumper. This late evening view in July 1981, showing it returning to town along Bell Road on the loop working through Park Wood estate. Note the former trolleybus traction poles still in use for street lighting.

It was not until March 1981 that the first new buses were delivered in this livery, but a revised application was applied, with the brown carried higher up the sides and a cream roof. Bedford chassis were again specified, but with Wadham Stringer 61-seat bodywork. One of the five, 181 (MKP 181W), was taken pulling out of the Hatherall Road terminus in June 1981, with a storm brewing over the North Downs.

Also joining the fleet in 1981 were two Duple bodied Bedford coaches that were delivered in dealer white. They were not identical; 184 had a roof-mounted destination blind, while 185 (PKE 185W) had an internal blind box fitted in the upper windscreen, which was particularly hard to read in daylight. It was more visible by night, as seen in this January 1982 view in the High Street. In the background, M&D's traditional liveried Atlantean was passing by on the service to Gillingham.

Also in 1981 two Bedford JJLs, with Marshall bodywork, came on hire. The JJL was a rear-engined low-floor midibus, which was considerably ahead of its time. It failed to attract any hard orders, so by this stage development work on this project had ceased and Marshall were seeking to find customers for the completed prototypes. The neat design and attractive white, orange and grey livery of EKX 648T is shown clearly in this July 1981 view. It had just worked an early morning commuter run to Maidstone East station and the driver had parked up in a section of Earl Street that did not normally see buses and gone to the enquiry office in Rose Yard. Honnors' shop (now Waterstone's) is decorated for the Royal Wedding.

The other JJL was HKX 553V, which carried a grey and white livery with a thin orange stripe. The position of the emergency door made the offside slightly less attractive than the nearside. In June 1981 it was working the Sunday circular service at Penenden Heath.

9 August 1981 saw the introduction of the Maidstone Area Bus Services (MABS) network, which finally co-ordinated the Maidstone Borough Council's and Maidstone & District's services. One of the sections of route that the borough buses generally ceased to serve was the London Road. On 1 August 1981 Wadham Stringer bodied Bedford 181 (MKP 181W) was at a stop in Headingly Road, on the London Road terminal loop, that would be served by the diversion of M&D's routes to Larkfield and beyond.

One of the few new facilities to feature in the MABS network was the commuter service from Barming Station to Barming, over a mile away from the station. On 16 August 1981, 213 (GRC 883N), a former Nottingham Leopard, now in Nile blue, was waiting in Hermitage Lane for returning commuters.

As a result of the scheme M&D closed its Maidstone depot and it resourced its workings from Borough Green, Tunbridge Wells, Hawkhurst, Gillingham and even East Kent at Ashford. While M&D retained many of its trunk routes, often extended or diverted into Maidstone estates, some rural routes were transferred to Maidstone Borough operations. This is the first of three shots taken on 1 September 1981, showing 168 (WKE 68S) arriving at Hollingbourne Church.

The former M&D service to Coxheath was covered by extending the Loose service and 166 (WKE 66S) was demonstrating the new order at Linton Corner. MBC worked most of the Coxheath service and indeed service 29 to Marden.

An example of a trunk route rerouted to serve a local estate was M&D's 333 to Sittingbourne and Faversham, which was diverted via Vinters Park. MBC did have one evening peak short working to Detling on this route. Ex Nottingham HNU 125N, a late survivor in lilac livery, approaches the Chiltern Hundreds roundabout on this working.

MBC had just one scheduled working on the London Road, a schooldays only morning peak trip from Larkfield on service 111. This November 1981 view shows Leopard 222 (HNU 122N) on this working at Grace Avenue. The second Maidstone Borough bus behind is Bedford 174 (AKK 174T), covering an M&D working on service 74, no doubt as the result of a vehicle failure.

Two more Bedford JJLs arrived in October 1981, and these both carried fleet livery. 334 (AVS 930T) had worked in from Hollingbourne on this evening view in Maidstone High Street on 10 September 1982. By this stage it had also gained the MABS logo under the driver's window.

The fourth JJL 335 (UKK 335X) had not previously been registered and was therefore the only one to have a Kentish registration. In April 1983, it was photographed at Barming Station on the evening commuter service. Unlike the Leopard in the earlier view on this route, the JJL was small enough to be able to turn in the station forecourt.

Sunday 10 January 1982 saw this Maidstone Borough Bedford covering M&D service 309 from Borough Green to Penenden Heath. It was on layover at the Penenden Heath terminus, another traditional route now largely served by M&D. The reason for the unusual working was that the garage doors at Borough Green were frozen shut!

1982 was another busy year, with thirteen vehicles arriving and wholesale withdrawals of early Bedfords and the Leyland Leopards. First to arrive were four more Wadham Stringer bodied Bedfords, but then came 160 (ABH 760X), a former demonstrator Wright bodied Bedford, which introduced another new bodybuilder to the fleet. On Sunday 23 April 1982, soon after arrival, I found it at the Gatland Lane terminus. At this time Sunday schedules involved extensive interworking of routes and the blind had already been changed before running empty to Barming Bull to pick up the Park Wood service.

Seven new Wright bodied Bedfords arrived in October 1982, and featured a slightly more attractive, less angular body style than 160. Five were 61-seaters in brown livery, as shown by 138 (CKM 138Y) when brand new in Lower Stone Street heading for Marden.

The final pair were 53-seaters in blue livery, but were normally used as buses. These buses were bodied in Northern Ireland and employed the seating used by Ulsterbus on longer distance services, which was no more than bus seats with the upholstery extended over the handrail, but not providing a head rest. Les Auger, another longstanding driver, was with a trainee driver in 143 (CKN 143Y) on the Sutton Road in April 1983.

Two demonstrators were tried during 1982; Dennis Lancet UPD 269X featured Wadham Stringer 45-seat bodywork. On 10 September 1982 it was leaving town for Park Wood, heavily loaded on a route that normally used 61-seaters. Despite a second visit in 1983 no orders were forthcoming.

Far more exciting was the appearance of this articulated Leyland, FHE 291V, recorded here at Queen's Monument heading for Gatland Lane on 20 September 1982. This vehicle was based on an underfloor chassis, produced by Leyland-DAB (its Danish subsidiary at the time) and many standard Leyland National body parts. It had 55 seats and 65 standing capacity. It ran for a month at Maidstone and received both fleetnames and MABS stickers during its stay.

A new venture that began from 26 May 1983 was the operation of an express coach service between Dover and Blackpool, jointly with Burnley & Pendle and Leicester, under the 'City Flyer' name. In all-white livery Bedford YMT/Duple 184 (PKE 184W) was passing Maidstone West Station on this service in June 1983. All the buildings behind were soon to be demolished for the Westborough Shopping Centre.

Maidstone's regular allocation included Bedford YMT/Duple 245 (TER 5S), which was purchased in April 1983 and last operated by Harwich and Dovercourt Coaches. It was photographed at London, Aldgate Bus Station, where this service called and connected with other municipal services to Reading and Southend. The 'City Flyer' logo was based on the Pendle Witch.

Another Bedford YMT/Duple purchased at the same time was 244 (SGS 505W), which came from Stephenson of Hullbridge, Essex. Unlike 245, it was repainted in blue coach livery and was pictured in Aldgate Bus Station in October 1983.

Wadham Stringer Vanguard bodied Bedford YMT 211 (TKM 111X), also gained 'City Flyer' vinyls, as a spare vehicle for this service. It was recorded in this condition on local bus work crossing Maidstone Bridge in October 1983.

Six Nottingham Leopards remained in the fleet long enough to be repainted in blue coach livery and 222 (HNU 122N) also gained 'City Flyer' lettering. This November 1983 view shows it in the depot yard.

The first allover advert bus in the fleet was Bedford YNQ/Wright 160 (ABH 760X), which was painted for Ward Construction, advertising new homes on the Grove Green estate, in February 1983. Freshly out of the paintshop, it was posing in the winter sun at Barming Bull Inn terminus.

Titan 26, which had been out of use in the depot since 1979, was restored, partially through the efforts of a group of enthusiastic staff, to mechanical fitness. By April 1983 it was in use outside the Archbishop's Palace dispensing old age pensioners' travel tokens. Bodywork restoration was still in progress, but hints of its original livery can be seen on some panels.

On the same duty a year later 26 had been fully restored to its original golden ochre livery, complete with painted Golden Shred adverts. This shade of brown was used from the mid-1950s and was a lighter and more attractive shade than the darker brown then being used for the bus fleet.

Another hired vehicle, which was operated from November 1983 to July 1984, was East Kent YKT 429V, a Ford A with Wadham Stringer 23-seat bodywork. This vehicle carried a special livery for a discontinued service linking the William Harvey Hospital at Ashford with parts of its rural catchment area. Ironically this view shows it on the short-lived Aylesford–Maidstone Hospital service, crossing the now replaced Bailey bridge at Aylesford in December 1983.

Another view of Duple Dominant bodied Bedford YMT 175 (AKK 175T) taken in South Park Road in April 1983, by which time it had lost its 75th anniversary plaque and sponsored adverts. This livery application was limited to just two Duple bodied buses, short 170 (WKE 70S) being the only other recipient.

Early in 1984 a Bedford YNT, with rare Wright Contour coachwork, joined the fleet and carried 'City Flyer' livery. Numbered 201 and initially registered A201 OKN, it was soon re-registered HKR 11, raided from the preserved trolleybus. In July 1984, it was tracked down in Burnley Bus Station.

A second Bedford YNT coach 202 (B202 XKR), this time with a Duple Laser body and in coach livery arrived in December 1984, but did not enter service until the following March. My first sighting of this vehicle was on Maundy Thursday, 4 April 1985 at Victoria Coach Station on a National Express relief to Paignton.

For nearly three months during the summer of 1985 this Alexander bodied Leyland Leopard (WRN 14R) was on hire from Burnley & Pendle. It was found on a local route at the Queen's Monument on 1 July.

A second allover advert had appeared in May 1985, when Wright bodied Bedford 238 (CKM 138Y) was repainted for Nottcutts Garden Centre. It was also at the Queen's Monument when photographed on 1 July 1985.

Operation of the Bedford JJLs in Maidstone was relatively short-lived. HKX 553V did not operate again in Maidstone after an accident in 1982 and the other three were hired to Brighton Borough from November 1983 and were eventually sold to them in 1985. They initially ran in a special livery and worked a service from the railway station to the shopping centre. This March 1984 view showed UKK 335X at Brighton station.

In 1985, Maidstone Borough took over the operation of the seasonal Seabus services previously run by Maidstone & District. They operated from the bus station and peak summer loadings resulted in the return of double-deck operation. This was achieved by the hire of SDM 97V, a Leyland Fleetline with a Northern Counties body, from Chester City Transport. It was pictured leaving Maidstone Bus Station on 13 July. This hire was repeated the following summer.

The only vehicle acquired during 1985 was 206 (JKX 726N), a low mileage, eleven-year old Bedford YMT Duple Dominant bus that had been a Vauxhall Motors development vehicle. On a grey day in December 1985 I recorded it on Maidstone Bridge.

Bedford Duple Dominant Express coach 277 (JKJ 277V) was repainted from light to dark blue in January 1985 and this view is showing it, still shiny, on layover in Lower Stone Street Bus Station in March of that year.

260 (ABH 260X), the short Bedford YNQ with Wright bodywork, was given its second repaint in July 1985 when its allover advert was replaced by fleet livery. By this stage the windscreen and destination areas had been rebuilt. It was pictured turning into Mill Street from the lower High Street in August 1985.

In 1985, a major effort began to eliminate the remaining few vehicles in the pale blue livery and the remaining Duple Dominant bodied Bedford YMTs were painted into brown livery applied in the same format as on the Wadham Stringer buses. 273 (AKK 173T) was running past Maidstone Museum in May 1986.

Two more Wright bodied Bedford YMTs came in 1986 and were the last new vehicles to enter service with Maidstone Borough Council. Despite being fitted with 53 dual-purpose seats, like CKN 142/3Y, this pair was in brown, rather than blue, livery. 203 (C203 GKR), in as new condition, passes a Talbot Avenger on Tonbridge Road in September 1986.

The next few shots show the fleet and operations in the run up to deregulation and the formation of Boro'line Maidstone. Several vehicles were partially repainted into the interim Boro'line livery, with the cream areas painted yellow and the addition of grey skirts. Wadham Stringer Vanguard bodied Bedford YMT, 210 (TKM 110X), with a Wright bodied example behind, was parked in Maidstone Bus Station on 25 October 1986, the last day before deregulation. Boro'line services did not use the bus station.

Bedford YMT/Wright 242 (CKN 142Y) was strangely repainted from blue and cream into brown, yellow and grey interim livery, while in true Boro'line fashion, sister 243 (CKN 143Y) gained full blue, yellow and grey livery. 242 was recorded at Park Avenue in September 1986.

Bedford/Duple 268 (WKE 68S – by now re-registered 4066 KO) was recorded in Tovil Green on 25 October 1986. The yellow poster on the side features 'Iggy', a marketing mascot based on the fossilised iguanadon found in Maidstone that is part of the town's coat of arms.

From Metrobus of Orpington, two Duple bodied Bedfords came on hire pending formal acquisition by Boro'line. Bus bodied XPL 889T was still in Metrobus livery when this picture was taken at the Queen's Monument on 12 October 1986.

The other vehicle was a Dominant II Express bodied coach, new to Eastern National. BNO 701T was found on the westbound stop at Queen's Monument on 25 October 1986. It had already received the yellow-lettered destination blind that was part of the new image.

BORO'LINE MAIDSTONE 1986–1992

D-Day, Sunday 26 October 1986 was a fine sunny day. In the depot yard, 242 (CKN 142Y) had now gained new Boro'line Maidstone fleetnames on its interim livery. Note also the broadside advert, which had appeared on several members of the fleet.

Also here was Bedford/Wadham Stringer 279 (MKP 179W) in full Boro'line colours. The fleetnames are freshly applied – the backing paper is discarded on the ground. The new image was designed by Ray Stenning's Best Impressions, which is the leading bus industry design company.

On service was 211 (TKM 111X), again in interim livery with the advert resulting in a truncated fleetname on the nearside. The location is Upper Stone Street, near the Barton Road junction.

A number of buses were hired pending new deliveries to operate the route network, which required both double-deckers and midibuses. From Ipswich Buses came a pair of Dodge 21-seaters; C204 WGV carried a quite attractive Northern Counties body and was recorded in Wheeler Street on an inward working of the Penenden Heath route. This road was previously unserved and one of several parts of the route that required smaller buses.

From East Kent came three Bristol LHSs with ECW bodies that were especially low (and narrow) for restricted routes, particularly to pass under Newtown Road railway-bridge in Ashford. Replaced at East Kent by minibuses, they were eventually purchased. GFN 562N was recorded leaving Maidstone Hospital.

A few weeks later GFN 559N was picking up at the Queen's Monument for Allington Way, which was again regularly served by borough buses after a five year absence. This was the only one of the three to have a white waistband.

On 30 November 1986, just days before returning to Ipswich the other Dodge, D202 YDX, with East Lancs bodywork, covered a Sunday run on the Park Wood service.

The same day saw the first of Boro'line's own batch of four of these vehicles, 235 (D235 MKK), work a journey from Penenden Heath along Church Street by Clarke's furnishing store, which was destroyed by fire in January 1995.

Bedford coach 285 (PKE 185W), delivered in dealer white, gained Nile blue coach livery in October 1985 which was modified a year later with small Boro'line fleetnames. It was picking up school children in Park Wood estate in December 1986.

Three new buses were delivered early in 1987. First to arrive was 207 (D207 MKK), a 55-seat Scania with East Lancs bodywork. At deregulation Boro'line gained operations on service 10 to Ashford, with a Sunday extension (under Kent County Council contract) to Folkestone. 207 was a regular on this service and it was seen at Folkestone Bus Station in July 1987, in the company of Hastings & District OWE 771K, a rare East Lancs bodied Bristol VR, new to Sheffield: it is now preserved in Sheffield livery.

Next to arrive were two double-deckers with the same combination of chassis and body make; these had celebrity status at the time for having the highest seating capacity in the country, a massive 92 seats. 212 (D212 MKK) was outside the Safeway supermarket in King Street, also on the Sunday service to Folkestone in June 1990.

In typical Boro'line practice they ran without fleetnames for a while, but when they were fitted, each had different coloured vinyl. Under the Christmas lights at the Queen's Monument in December 1990, 213 (D213 MKK) was showing its red front fleetname, while 212 had a blue one.

Regular double-deck operation returned with the hire of four Leyland Atlanteans, with East Lancs bodies from Eastbourne Buses, from October 1986. In February 1987, KHC 812K was passing the Safeway supermarket in King Street on its way to Senacre Wood.

Meanwhile, there were several developments in the coaching fleet. October 1986 saw a former Scania demonstrator, with Plaxton bodywork, enter service as No. 205. This was C92 DTM, which carried yet another livery of dark blue with light blue relief. My July 1987 view was taken in Mill Street, Maidstone.

A new Scania coach to the same specification (but with the high floor version of the body) was 204, which gained the registration 4066 KO, and carried full fleet livery. It was recorded at Portsmouth on another M&D and East Kent Bus Club trip on 20 June 1987.

A few minutes later came Bedford coach 214 (BNO 701T), by now repainted in full fleet livery, albeit with a different application to suit the lines of its Duple bodywork. It was working a summer Saturday National Express service 723 from Dartford to Ventnor, normally operated by Boro'line.

The fourth vehicle in the batch of East Kent Bristol LHSs, GFN 561N, arrived as a purchase in November 1986 and was numbered 261. It had been in use as a staff bus for Kent Engineering at Canterbury (formerly the East Kent Central Works) and came in this red, blue and silver livery. Maidstone Hospital is the venue of this February 1987 shot.

Five ex Ribble Leyland Tigers joined the fleet for the 1987 season. They were in white, and four carried black skirts; all had a variety of fleetnames. 220 (A126 MBA) had yellow/red on the offside, as shown in this August 1987 depot view, while that on the near side was all red. At this time the depot was used on Saturdays for a Park & Ride car park, which was useful for getting access and photographs, as spare vehicles would be parked in the yard, rather than in the garage.

Another member of the same batch at Epsom Downs for the 1990 Derby, 223 (A123 MBA) shows a white fleetname at the top of the windscreen, while the sides had the blue/red version.

On Sunday 7 June 1987, through the good offices of Operations Director, Norman Kemp, three of the four Bristol LHSs were lined up in the depot yard. Two had been painted in base colours for allover adverts and the missing one was away being painted.

Also posed for pictures in Armstrong Road was recently arrived Bedford/Duple coach 216 (562 PTU), which came from Highfield of Wigan and was an executive coach with only 42 seats, tables and a toilet.

New the previous month, Leyland Lynx 228 (D156 HML) was pictured from the fire-escape steps, before working the 10 to Folkestone. It was the middle bus in a batch of three.

Duple Laser bodied Bedford 202 (B202 XKM) was arriving at Eastbourne on a day tour on 6 August 1987, showing Boro'line names on the old livery.

Another used coach purchased was 217 (A776 JBG), a Volvo B10M with Duple Carribbean style body. It ran in this blue and orange livery, but lasted only a year in the fleet.

On 23 August 1987, Boro'line supplied rail replacement buses between Maidstone West and Paddock Wood. Just leaving East Farleigh station was short Bedford/Wright 260 (ABH 260X), now in fleet livery. A nice touch was the use of service number 61, the correct headcode for trains on this line.

Some of the surviving Duple Dominant bodied Bedford buses gained the blue Boro'line livery, as exemplified by 276 (AKK 176T) turning into Romney Place in March 1987.

The four Dodges gained revised vinyls in 1987, with yellow/white replaced by white/red. 235 (D235 MKK) showed its new image in June 1987 as it travelled along Palace Avenue.

Another Kent County Council tendered service was Sunday 22 from Bromley to Tunbridge Wells, which ran every two hours and required two buses. 288 (Q288 JKO) was working the service at Sevenoaks Bus Station on 18 October 1987, two days after the great hurricane that made it 'Oneoak'.

During the autumn of 1987 two open-top Leyland Titans came on hire from Brighton Transport, mainly for driver training. It was reported that they did make some appearances in service at peak times (with the upper deck closed off!) and this was supported by the Park Wood route number on the blind in this depot view of LUF 133F on 5 December 1987.

Ex Metrobus Bedford 215 (XPL 889T) received an allover advertisement for Sandell Perkins in June 1987. The East Kent garage forecourt at Ashford, which at that time served as the terminus for some rural routes, was the location for this April 1988 view.

1988 saw the first of the London contracts, but with delivery of the fourteen Leyland Olympians for these routes running late, twelve Roe bodied Leyland Atlanteans were hired from Kingston-upon-Hull City Transport. Some ran initially in Maidstone, like WAG 376X recorded at the Senacre Wood terminus on 2 January 1988.

The first day of the contract was Saturday 16 January 1988 and NAT 341M was working service 233 (Eltham–Swanley) at Sidcup. Boro'line fleetnames and London Bus logos had been added.

Also on the first day of operation and WAG 382X was standing at the layover area at Bexleyheath after working service 132 from Eltham. Note the erroneous space in the destination blind.

Eltham Station was the focus of the Boro'line London operation and the other routes were circulars 228 and 328. WAG 379X is on 328 in this sunny view on 29 February 1988.

Also at Eltham Station on the same day was 751 (E151 OMD) the first of the batch of Optare bodied Leyland Olympians. The blue was carried around the front of these vehicles, unlike most of the Maidstone fleet, which had yellow fronts.

A further hire for the London routes was a single Leyland Atlantean from Greater Manchester. LJA 631P featured Northern Counties bodywork and was used from January to May 1988. There was no shortage of fleetnames carried in this April 1988 view, as it was standing spare at Eltham Station.

With the opening of the London base, operation of Sunday service 22 was transferred from Maidstone. On 6 March 1988, new Olympian 753 (E153 OMD) was leaving Tonbridge for Tunbridge Wells.

Delayed delivery resulted in the last three Optare bodied Olympians being cancelled and in their place came two Scanias and a Volvo. Representing the pair of Scanias with Alexander bodies is 702 (E702 XKR), in dealer stock white, at Eltham Station on 26 March 1988.

The underfloor-engined Volvo Citybus took the fleet number and registration number intended for the last of the Olympians. Also on 26 March 1988, 764 (E164 OMD) turned from the main street in Eltham towards the station. It was the last chassis built by Volvo at the Irvine factory and it carried an Ailsa badge on the front grille. It was received in this white plus blue stripe livery.

Meanwhile, in Maidstone strange vehicles continued to appear on hire. In late May 1988, four Seddon Pennines with Alexander bodies came on two months hire from Clydeside Scottish. On 4 June 1988, DSD 537V was pictured turning into Station Road on the Saturday Park & Ride service to Springfield, which used the car park at the Kent County Council offices.

The same day saw NDP 41R, a long Bristol VR with Northern Counties bodywork, newly arrived from Reading Buses and found in the depot yard. Four of these vehicles worked in Maidstone during the summer of 1988.

Star vehicle of 1988 was this former Southdown full fronted Leyland Titan PD3 that entered service in June in full fleet livery. 290 (originally BUF 278C, but registered 217 UKL soon after entering service in Maidstone) was found in Lower Stone Street on 17 December 1988 and (despite the destination display) was on the Park & Ride service to the Armstrong Road depot. This vehicle is now preserved.

Bristol LHS 259 (GFN 559N) was displaying its Broadway Bistro advert on an inward working on the London Road service at the Buckland Lane stop in June 1988.

All four Bristol LHSs carried allover adverts, but only 263 (GFN 560N) had a coloured base livery. The advertiser in this case was Bourne's estate agents. This vehicle was taken in Cumberland Avenue on Shepway estate in January 1988.

More midibuses came on hire from August 1988 in the form of four MCW Metrorider 25-seaters from Northumbria. Before the days of Sunday shopping small vehicles were of sufficient size to operate the few services running. Three of these vehicles (E830/2/3 BTN) were working the hourly group of services at the Queen's Monument on 25 September 1988.

Part way through the hire period there was an exchange of vehicles, as the vehicles at Maidstone, which were fitted with luggage boots, were required for London Express duties at Kentish Bus. They were replaced by examples with no boots, like E809 BTN in King Street on 27 October 1988.

Boro'line's own Metroriders arrived in October 1988, allowing the return of the hired examples. First of the batch 251 (F997 EKM) was heading for West Farleigh in Lower Stone Street on 17 December 1988.

From 19 November 1988 a new contract took Boro'line buses into central London, with the operation of service 188 between Euston and Greenwich. Needless to say the new buses for this route were late and operation commenced with hired buses from Ipswich and Nottingham. Ipswich WPV 87L, a Leyland Atlantean with a Roe body, was found at Elephant & Castle on 23 November. Initially up to nine were hired from Ipswich and up to four buses remained until early 1991.

Representing the eight Nottingham vehicles, Northern Counties bodied Daimler Fleetline PAU 196R was turning round the war memorial in Euston Bus Station on 24 November. The unusual body styling was to Nottingham's own design.

The use of Nottingham vehicles did not last as long as the Ipswich ones, but it did continue well into 1989. Nottingham Fleetline, PAU 199R, was heading for Greenwich through Elephant & Castle on 21 February 1989.

Problems with the operation of London Buses' Bexleybus operation resulted in Boro'line taking over at short notice the running of two more routes from 26 November 1988. To resource this, ten Leyland Nationals were hired from London Country North East. National green liveried LPB 210P working route 422 had arrived at Bexleyheath on the first day of operation.

Although all from the same source, the ten vehicles came from four different batches and carried three different liveries. UPD 338S displays the post privatisation livery adopted by LCNE.

Still on the first day, but at the Woolwich end of the route, TPD 172M displays the light green band on National green livery that was used as a quick way of changing the old National Bus Company image.

The second route was the 492 running between Bexleyheath and Dartford. Also on 26 November 1988 was AYR 345T, one of four Nationals acquired from London Buses; it was pictured at Dartford Station.

A view taken in the Crayford yard on Sunday 4 December 1988, with Ipswich Leyland Atlantean HDX 904N to the fore. Behind can be seen the rear of a former Southend Fleetline (TGX 820M) hired from Ensign, Purfleet for driver training. Between them is NSP 314R, one of the former Tayside Volvo Ailsas – eight were purchased and this was one of a pair that Ensign had repainted and used briefly on its own services in the Romford and Ilford areas.

From time to time vehicles worked from the wrong depots. My first sighting of a Crayford Leyland National on service in Maidstone took place on 17 December 1988, when BYV 436V was found on the Park Wood service in Lower Stone Street.

The Volvo Ailsas all entered service in full livery, again with blue fronts, and NSP 318R shows the standard livery form as it departed Bexleyheath on 7 January 1989.

Typical of the detail differences in the Boro'line fleet NSP 316R displays a smaller size fleetname and no red stripe. It was the only one to carry this variation and was also recorded on the same day as the view above.

The fourteen Volvo Citybuses with Alexander bodies were delivered in March and April 1989, allowing the release of some of the hired vehicles from Nottingham and Ipswich. 912 (F112 TML) was awaiting passengers at the Greenwich terminus (with the *Cutty Sark* behind) on 31 October 1990.

Another Leyland Titan joined the fleet in March 1988 for use as a driver training bus. This was a former Bournemouth Corporation Weymann bodied example. New in 1950, it had been preserved and was initially used in Bournemouth livery. Numbered 299, its original registration (KEL 128) was transferred to a coach and it became XKP 782A. It gained full fleet livery early in 1989.

Hire of a few Ipswich Atlanteans continued after the arrival of the Volvo Citybuses for route 188 and their use moved to other routes. On 20 May 1989, TRT 95M, devoid of fleetnames and with a crude 422 penned on the blind display, was photographed at Bexleyheath.

Maidstone buses could often be found at Crayford and were normally used for staff shuttles between the depot and Bexleyheath or Eltham. Their use in service was more rare, but not unknown. Also on 20 May 1989, advert liveried Bedford 272 (AKK 172T) was working on 492.

245 (TER 5S)'s original Duple coach body was scrapped in 1987 and the chassis stood forlornly in the depot yard for many months. It re-entered service in May 1989 with a new Willowbrook Warrior 61-seat body. On 10 June 1989, it was working a rural free bus that provided shopping facilities for OAPs in the borough, in the days before universal free travel for the over 60s.

201 (HKR 11) the Wright Contour bodied Bedford got a full repaint in Boro'line livery in late 1987. It was found in the Maidstone depot yard on 9 April 1989.

Early in 1988 the coach fleet gained two Leyland Royal Tigers with Van Hool bodies from Travellers of Hounslow. 231 (B348 AMH) was caught in the depot yard on the last day of 1988. Both vehicles gained fleet livery early in 1989.

I was a passenger on the same vehicle on 23 March 1990 on a private hire trip to France. The rather bleak location of this view is the off-season sea front at Le Touquet-Paris-Plage.

Also in 1988, two other Royal Tigers with Plaxton coachwork came from Grey-Green of London. 286 (originally A849 UYM) gained the registration KEL 128 from the ex-Bournemouth Titan purchased for driver training, as shown in this view at Epsom for the 1990 Derby.

Another brace of Van Hool bodied Leyland Royal Tigers came from Travellers in 1989. These two were painted white with a yellow band as shown by 292 (D123 HMT), about to board the Sally Line ferry at Ramsgate in March 1991.

Two more coach purchases came in late 1988 from Bebb, Llantwit Fadre. They were Bedford YNTs with Duple Laser bodies and both were repainted in fleet livery prior to entering service in early 1989. 209 (B46 DNY) was taken on Epsom Downs for the 1990 Derby.

The other one of the pair 208 (B48 DNY) was spotted on 12 January 1990, at Park Wood shops, while making a rare appearance on local bus work.

Another 1988 arrival was from Lancaster City Transport, in the form of a 12-seat Ford Transit minibus registered PCW 511X. Numbered 246, it ran for a while in Lancaster's white with blue stripes livery, but gained fleet livery in November 1988. It was photographed at the southern end of the Chequers bus road in September 1991.

In 1989, four more Ford Transits, with 16-seat bodywork came from Alder Valley for school contracts in the Dartford area. They were also used on crew shuttle work and 980 (D318 WPE) was undertaking a driver change at Eltham Station in July 1990.

Returning to bus operations, another new London Transport route (108 Lewisham–Wanstead) began on 25 November 1989. A new base was opened in Greenwich for this route, with the 188 buses transferred here from Crayford. Twelve more Leyland Lynxes were obtained to work this route and the last of these 812 (G45 VME) was photographed in the old Lewisham Bus Station in November 1990.

In December 1989, a further MCW Metrorider numbered 249 (F241 JVW) arrived from Chambers of Stevenage and entered service without repaint. It was operating on the Springfield Park & Ride service at Week Street on 6 January 1990.

Former Metrobus Bedford/Duple bus 215 (XPL 889T) was a vehicle that never carried fleet livery. It gained its second allover advert livery in June 1989, which was jointly sponsored by Happy Homes and Wilkins Butchers. It was waiting to depart for Ashford in this July 1989 view at the Queen's Monument stop.

A number of vehicles carried broadside adverts as exemplified by 266 (WKE 66S), which carried them from 1985 until it was sold in 1990. It is shown swinging into the High Street from Fairmeadow in July 1989, with a glimpse of fleet livery on the front and lower bodyside, beneath the display for Computerwise Insurance.

The hire of Ipswich Atlanteans continued with four vehicles generally in use until early 1991. They also made odd appearances in service at Maidstone, including when this shot of Ipswich 94 (TRT 94M) was taken in November 1989. Despite the lack of destination blind, a few passengers have been gathered on the run from Maidstone Hospital.

Further school contracts were obtained from April 1990 and four Leyland Fleetlines, ex West Midlands Travel and in dealer white, entered the fleet as a result. 264 (MOM 579P) was the only one with Park Royal bodywork and it was seen heading for Barming at the Cannon stop soon after arrival at Maidstone.

Metro-Cammell-Weymann bodied example 265 (KON 315P) in Wat Tyler Way on the approach to the town centre on 28 November 1990. It is queuing in the pre-Christmas Saturday shopping traffic – at this time Maidstone had a serious shortage of parking spaces.

2 September 1990 saw Ken Morgan's Bygone Buses begin competing on local routes. A former driver, Ken had previously run River Valley Coaches and Bygone Buses was originally formed to operate a 1949 Bedford OB and an ex London Routemaster. Operations began with just two buses, but by the end of the year a small network was in operation with four buses. On 22 December 1990, MCW bodied Fleetline 267 (NOC 389R) was recorded ahead of a pair of Bygone Buses at the Queen's Monument. The ex M&D Bristol VR (GKL 826N) was driven by Ken Morgan.

On 1 December 1990, Wright bodied Bedford 243 (CKN 143Y) was waiting at Coxheath. Behind was Bygone Buses Leyland National (GAE 371N), which was driven by Trevor Turner, another former driver and Ken Morgan's son-in-law. Trevor later ran buses under his own name and continues as a coach operator today.

Back to the Queen's Monument, this time on 15 December 1990, and Boro'line were using demonstrator H220 TCP, a DAF with Hungarian Ikarus bodywork on the Senacre Wood service; note the east European black on white number blind. The same Bygone Buses Bristol VR lurks behind.

Meanwhile, on the coaching front, three Van Hool bodied DAFs were the only vehicles to join the fleet in 1990. 293 (G970 KJX), seen here passing Maidstone Museum, and sister 294 carried a white-based livery.

Final member of the batch 295 (G972 KJX) carried full fleet livery and was photographed in Castle Way, Leybourne in July 1991. These leased vehicles left at the end of the season, after a short stay at Maidstone.

Conductor operation returned in Maidstone in 1988, using both the preserved Titan and the former Southdown example. Initially their use on normal service was limited to covering vehicle shortages, but later became regular in response to the Bygone Buses using their Routemaster on local services. On 4 May 1990, 26 (26 YKO) was photographed at the Coxheath (Wilsons Lane/Gallants Lane) terminus, which today is described as East Farleigh.

11 June 1991 saw the introduction of a permanent Park & Ride service then numbered 503 to Coombe Quarry, which replaced the previous Saturday operations using the nearby depot in Armstrong Road. At the Coombe Quarry site was short and narrow 23-seat Metrorider 255 (E52 HFE), one of three on long-term hire from Grimsby-Cleethorpes Transport.

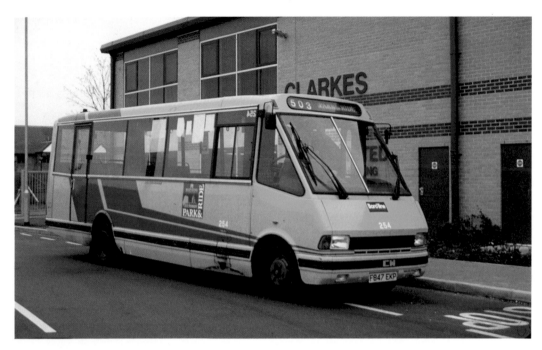

The second bus on Coombe Quarry route on 1 December 1990 was Maidstone's own long and narrow 28-seat Metrorider 254 (F847 EKP), which had been repainted in the dedicated Park & Ride livery in June 1990.

The other vehicle in livery for the Coombe Quarry service was long and wide 33-seat Metrorider 249 (217 UKL ex F241 JWV), which was photographed on 26 September 1991.

All three Grimsby-Cleethorpes Metroriders were painted into fleet livery in late 1990 and 256 (E54 HFE) was photographed at Leeds Church on 23 March 1991. They were the only vehicles hired from another operator to be repainted, but the hire ended after July 1991.

Earlier the same day, 255 (E52 HFE) was recorded at Boxley on service 30, a Saturday only KCC tendered operation to Hempstead Valley and Rainham, a route that was run commercially on Mondays to Fridays by Roseway Buses.

One more Metrorider in the fleet was a 28-seat coach bodied example, which arrived in December 1989. Numbered 250, it originally was registered G298 SKP, but in March 1991 it was re-registered to HKR 11 upon the sale of its previous holder. It carried a white livery with a tiny fleetname and was found in King Street in September 1991.

Meanwhile, Crayford based Scania 701 (E701 XKR) gained allover adverts for Crayford Motors in September 1989. Here 701 (E701 XKR) had just arrived at the Swanley, Beechenlea Lane terminus of 233 on 28 July 1990.

January 1991 saw the arrival of more new vehicles for London routes, on this occasion to update the fleet, rather than for new routes. Six Leyland Olympians, with Northern Counties bodywork, displaced the Volvo Ailsas. 767 (H767 EKJ) was pictured at Bexleyheath on 8 March 1991. This batch was delivered with slightly different shades of paint (perhaps from a different supplier), with the blue much darker.

Four Leyland Lynx 2s replaced the Leyland Nationals on service 492 and 815 (H815 HKJ) is seen arriving at Dartford on 13 March 1991.

A little over a year after the end of the hire of Nottingham Fleetlines for London routes, more Nottingham vehicles came in September 1990, this time for use in Maidstone. The vehicles were East Lancs bodied Leyland Atlanteans, but still to the standard Nottingham style, as shown by my shot of 271 (GVO 722N). It was on rail replacement work at Maidstone East on 1 December 1990.

Four vehicles arrived in September 1990, two N-reg examples were purchased and two M-reg ones were initially hired, but purchased soon after and all four gained fleet colours during the autumn. 273 (OTO 559M) was seen in Bicknor Road, Park Wood on 23 March 1991.

From January 1991 the turbocharger whine of the Volvo Ailsa returned to the streets of Maidstone, unheard since the demise of M&D's examples in 1983. On the 19th of that month, 918 (NSP 322R) was heading for Senacre Wood, still displaying London Transport roundels.

Two Volvo Ailsas were cannibalised for spares, but the other six continued in frontline use in Maidstone, often on the Senacre Wood service in competition with Bygone Buses, which had now developed operations that required ten buses in service around Maidstone. In King Street on 2 October 1991, 915 (NSP 316R) was on such a working.

The four Leyland Nationals also entered service at Maidstone and 903 (BYW 380V) was found at Headcorn on 2 April 1991 on the annual concessionary token issuing duty. It was the first National to be withdrawn later that year.

The same day saw Leyland Lynx 2 demonstrator H733 HWK at work in Maidstone turning at the Cannon, between trips on the Senacre Wood service, which at this time was being heavily duplicated to counter Bygone Buses operations. Although only used for two weeks it gained fleetnames.

Following the earlier demonstration, four DAF SB220/Ikarus vehicles came on lease in August 1991. 222 (J997 GCP) was located in Padsole Lane on 26 September 1991, displaying the white based livery that all four initially carried.

From 4 November 1991 a further Park & Ride site opened on the London Road and the service was linked to the Coombe Quarry facility and operation converted to full size vehicles. As a result, a number of vehicles were painted into Park & Ride livery, including three of this batch in September and October 1991. 220 (J995 GCP) was at the London Road terminus on 8 February 1992; my wife was paying for the ticket as I took this picture.

To complete the Park & Ride fleet two other buses were also repainted and I photographed both of these on 14 December 1991. Leyland Lynx 227 (D155 HML) was about to turn from Loose Road into Armstrong Road as it nears the Coombe Quarry car park.

Elderly Duple bodied Bedford 275 (794 SKO ex AKK 175T) was an unlikely vehicle for this high profile operation and was indeed on a Hospital–Park Wood working in this view, at the junction of Fairmeadow and High Street, also on 14 December 1991.

Another KCC tendered operation was for extra journeys on M&D's service 151 between Chatham and West Malling, and is illustrated by this view taken on 2 October 1991 in Military Road, Chatham. Bedford/Wright 243 (CKN 143Y) was almost in full livery, but lacking the red stripe.

An eclectic selection of Boro'line Maidstone vehicles at Maidstone Hospital on 31 October 1991, led by Metrorider 254 (F847 FKP) now displaced from Park & Ride duties, on a short-lived service via London Road. Behind is 284 (PKE 184W) a Bedford/Duple coach, which received full livery in May 1988 and had spent a creditable ten years in the fleet. A Volvo Ailsa brings up the rear.

Carrying its fifth and final livery during its ten years of service in the fleet, the sole short Bedford YNQ/Wright 260 (851 PKJ, ex ABH 760X), was repainted from the brown-based interim livery to full livery in May 1988. In September 1991, it was recorded departing the town for East Farleigh via Loose on service 88.

On 14 December 1991, a pair of Volvo Ailsas pass in Cumberland Avenue, with 315 (NSP 322R) heading for town. The reason for this visit to the depths of Shepway was to photograph the competing Maidstone & District services, which started on 2 December 1991 and further increased the competitive pressure on Boro'line Maidstone, already weakened by losses in London and the presence of Bygone Buses in Maidstone.

On the same day, Wright bodied Bedford 203 (C203 GKR), displaying full livery, was found in Park Way. The newly erected M&D bus stop can be seen at the front of the bus, while the Boro'line stop can be glimpsed through the windows of the bus.

Christmas Eve 1991 was a fine sunny day and the next few pictures provide an overview of operations at this time. Two more Leyland Atlanteans came from Nottingham in December 1991 and both ran in Nottingham colours as shown by 210 (OTO 541M) on the Tovil service in King Street.

Scania 212 (D212 MKK) had been repainted in August 1991 into the London-style application, with the blue area extended around the front. The orange window bill on the M&D Bristol VR behind shows it was running on one of the new local services.

To counter M&Ds competitive routes in Maidstone, Boro'line introduced two Monday to Friday services in the Medway Towns from 15 December 1991. However, from 20 December they were banned from the Pentagon Bus Station and banished to Military Road, from where Lynx 229 (D157 HML) was departing.

DAF 223 (J998 GCP), also at the same stop, was by this stage the only member of the batch of four not to be in Park & Ride livery. It was eventually repainted in April 1992, to replace the Lynxes in this livery repossessed in March 1992, only to go the same way in early May.

288 (Q288 JKO) swings into Military Road on the same day. Note another error in the paint shop; the boundary between the blue and yellow was set at the previous level between the brown and cream, but should have been higher to allow all of the fleetname to be on the blue background.

The second of the pair of Nottingham Leyland Atlanteans was acquired in December 1991 to resource competitive routes in Medway; 211 (OTO 546M) was photographed as it arrived in Maidstone High Street on 29 December 1991.

Towards the end of operations the same vehicle, still in Nottingham livery, but with the addition of fleet names, was picking up at the Queen's Monument on 11 April 1992. It had been pressed into service with partially completed accident repairs, no doubt as the result of vehicle shortages following repossessions.

Meanwhile, the London operation was sold to Kentish Bus from 17 February 1992, complete with 57 vehicles. Kentish Bus were well placed to take over these services. Former Operations Director, Norman Kemp had moved from Maidstone four years earlier to be Commercial Manager, responsible for Business Development, at Proudmutual-owned Kentish Bus, and as a result was not wholly unfamiliar with the Crayford depot arrangements or parts of the route portfolio! Northern Counties bodied Leyland Olympian 769 (H769 HKJ), with Kentish Bus names, was pictured at Bexleyheath on 1 August 1992.

This view of Optare bodied Leyland Olympian 762 (F991 UME) was taken at Woolwich on 18 March 1992. This vehicle had a strange history, being one of three vehicles cancelled in 1988, following delays in delivery. When completed all three were offered for sale via dealers and two passed to London Cityrama as E963/4 PME. The third vehicle was still in stock a year later when Boro'line were looking for additional vehicles and eventually it joined the fleet in June 1989.

From 5 January 1992 M&D introduced services to Penenden Heath and Tovil to complete their coverage of the town routes. On 11 May 1992, competing buses on the Penenden Heath service were awaiting custom at King Street.

On the same day Bedford/Duple Laser coach 202 (642 WKR ex B202 XKM) was covering the Park & Ride service following the enforced return of the four DAFs in livery for this service.

The final view of a Boro'line vehicle in use is of coach 216 (562 PTU) in the one-way system over the River Medway on 12 May 1992. It had been painted into base white, prior to disposal, but as an owned vehicle it was retained after the loss of leased vehicles and continued in use until the bitter end on 29 May 1992.

M&D took over 43 owned vehicles (plus the recovery truck) and the offices and depot in Armstrong Road. Two coaches were retained for their New Enterprise subsidiary, but the rest of the fleet were quickly sold. Twelve went to local dealer Wealden PSV at Five Oak Green. Two Bedford buses were standing in their depot on 3 July 1992, with JKX 726N showing evidence of running for the Wealden Beeline operating arm on its service 252 (Heathfield–Tunbridge Wells). Between these two buses can be seen XSA 4Y, the unique Dennis Lancet with Alexander Y-type bodywork.

The three repossessed Leyland Lynxes passed to Kentish Bus in April 1992 and were reunited with other former Boro'line vehicles. They were quickly painted into Kentish Bus livery and regularly worked route 227 Crystal Palace to Bromley, as shown by this view of D155 HML taken at Bromley North Station in September 1992.

Also repossessed at the same time was Metrorider 249 (217 UKL ex F241 JWV). It was obtained by Kentish Bus in June 1992 and further re-registered to F932 LKE. It was photographed at Aldgate Bus Station also in September 1992, in the company of a Reading Transport Leyland Olympian.

Some local reminders of Boro'line operations continued for many years. Leyland National AYR 345T was sold by Wealden PSV to Nu-Venture, Aylesford in October 1992 and lasted until 1999. This picture was taken on 30 July 1993 and shows it on its regular haunt, service 78 to Barming via Queen's Road.

British Bus purchased the Proudmutual group (including Kentish Bus) in 1994 and Maidstone & District in 1995, which was in turn purchased by the Cowie group in 1996 and became Arriva in 1997. Former Boro'line buses in the Kentish Bus fleet were dispersed far and wide, but one of the first transfers saw Lynx G45 VME sent to Maidstone in September 1995 for Park & Ride duties. It was standing at the Queen's Monument in Maidstone on 11 May 1996.

Fleet List 1974–1992

This fleet list is in abridged format and it ignores such complexities as vehicles being hired by Maidstone Borough Council prior to eventual purchase (often with temporary 400 series fleet numbers) and equally buses that worked on hire to other operators before sale. The history of the Bedford JJLs is particularly complex in this respect. HKX553V was withdrawn after an accident before obtaining its permanent number 331, while the other three spent over two years on hire to Brighton Borough before sale in 1985. The many demonstrator and hired vehicles are not listed, nor are cars and other service vehicles.

A fleet renumbering took place in January 1980, resulting in Bedfords having 100 and Leylands having 200 added to their fleet numbers. At the same time the two Dial a Ride Transits, previously unnumbered, became 331/2 in a series used for minibuses. In practice the use of fleet-number plates on much of the fleet resulted in old numbers being retained on vehicles. A further renumbering took place in April 1983, which put all buses in the 200 series. Preserved Titan 26 physically retained this number despite on paper becoming firstly 430 and then 226.

EXPLAINATION OF BODY CODES:

The first letters represents the type of vehicle – B = single-deck bus, C = coach, DP = dual purpose (ie coach seats in bus shell or vv), F = full front (on a chassis that would normally have a half-cab front), H = Highbridge double-deck bus.

The numbers show the seating capacity, on double-deckers the first figure gives upper-deck seating followed by the lower-deck capacity.

Final letters give entrance position and other information – D = dual entrance, F = front entrance, R = rear entrance, T = toilet fitted.

MAIDSTONE BOROUGH COUNCIL 1974 – 1986

Fleet No.	Reg. No.	Chassis	Date Body
8	998 AKT	Leyland Titan PD2/30	1957 Massey H33/28R
10-2	410-2 DKM	Leyland Titan PD2/30	1958 Massey H33/28R
13-5	413-5 GKT	Leyland Titan PD2/30	1959 Massey H33/28R
16-8	516-8 RKR	Leyland Titan PD2A/30	1960 Massey H33/28R
19-22	19-22 UKK	Leyland Titan PD2A/30	1962 Massey H33/28R
23-6	23-6 YKO	Leyland Titan PD2A/30	1963 Massey H33/28R
27-34	EKP 227-34C	Leyland Atlantean PDR1/1	1965 Massey H43/31F
35-42	JKE 335-42E	Leyland Atlantean PDR1/1	1967 Massey H43/31F
43	NKK 243F	Leyland Atlantean PDR1/1	1968 Massey H43/31F
44	OKJ 844F	Leyland Atlantean PDR1/1	1968 Massey H43/31F
45/6	OKM 145/6G	Leyland Atlantean PDR1/1	1968 Massey H43/31F
47-50	AKE 147-50K	Leyland Atlantean PDR1A/1	1971 Northern Counties H43/31F
51-54	EKR 151-5L	Leyland Atlantean AN68/1R	1972 Northern Counties H43/31F

8/10-54 all ex Maidstone Corporation Transport Department 1974

Fleet No.	Reg. No.	Chassis	Date Body
55-58	HKJ 255-8N	Bedford YRQ	1975 Willowbrook 001 B45F
59-61	JKN 59-61N	Bedford YRQ	1975 Willowbrook 001 B45F
62-4	JKO 62-4N	Bedford YRT	1975 Duple Dominant B53F
1-2	NKE 301-2P	Bedford YRT	1976 Duple Dominant Express C51F

NKE 302P to C53F 1981

Fleet No.	Reg. No.	Chassis	Date Body
3	NKE 303P	Bedford YRQ	1975 Duple Dominant B45F

Ex Duple demonstrator 1976

Fleet No.	Reg. No.	Chassis	Date Body
4-7	NKE 304-7P	Bedford YRT	1976 Duple Dominant B53F
	HOR 334/5L	Ford Transit	1972 Strachan Pacemaker B16F

Ex Freeman (Denis Hire Cars), Maidstone 1976

Fleet No.	Reg. No.	Chassis	Date Body
13-15	GRC 883-5N	Leyland Leopard PSU3B/4R	1975 Duple Dominant Express C51F
16	HNU 126N	Leyland Leopard PSU3B/4R	1975 Duple Dominant Express C51F

17-22	HNU 117-22N	Leyland Leopard PSU3B/4R	1975 Duple Dominant Express C49F
23-5	HNU 123-5N	Leyland Leopard PSU3B/4R	1975 Duple Dominant Express B53F
28	JCH 398N	Leyland Leopard PSU3B/4R	1975 Duple Dominant Express B53F

13-25/28 all ex City of Nottingham 1976/7

11	SKN 491R	Bedford YRT	1977 Willowbrook 001 B53F
65-9	WKE 65-9S	Bedford YMT (automatic)	1978 Duple Dominant B61F

WKE 68S to 4066 KO 1984

70	WKM 70S	Bedford YLQ (automatic)	1977 Duple Dominant B45F

Ex Duple demonstrator 1978

71-6	AKK 171-6T	Bedford YMT (automatic)	1978 Duple Dominant B61F
29	STD 119L	Leyland Leopard PSU3B/4R	1972 Pennine B47F

Ex Lancaster City Council 1979

212	STD 121L	Leyland Leopard PSU3B/4R	1972 Pennine B47F

Ex Lancaster City Council 1980

333	HKN 333V	Ford Transit	1980 Reeve Burgess DP17F
177/8	JKJ 277/8V	Bedford YMT	1979 Duple Dominant II Express C53F

stored until 1980

336	MKP 336W	Ford Transit	1980 Reeve Burgess DP17F
179-83	MKP 179-83W	Bedford YMT (automatic)	1981 Wadham Stringer Vanguard B61F
184-5	PKE 184-5W	Bedford YMT	1981 Duple Dominant II Express C53F
331	EKX 648T	Bedford JJL	1978 Marshall B24F
453	HKX 553V	Bedford JJL	1978 Marshall B24F
334	AVS 903T	Bedford JJL	1978 Marshall B27F
335	UKK 335X	Bedford JJL	1978 Marshall B27F

331, 453, 334/5 all ex Marshall, Cambridge 1981

108-11	TKM 108-11X	Bedford YMT	1982 Wadham Stringer Vanguard B61F
160	ABH 760X	Bedford YMQ (automatic)	1982 Wright TT B45F

Ex Shaw & Kilburn (dealer) 1982

137-41	CKM 137-41Y	Bedford YMT	1982 Wright TT B61F
142-3	CKN 142-3Y	Bedford YMT	1982 Wright TT DP53F
232	CKN 332Y	Bedford YMQS (automatic)	1982 Lex Maxeta B37F

Ex Bedford demonstrator 1982

245	TER 5S	Bedford YMT	1978 Duple Dominant II C53F

Ex Harwich & Dovercourt Coaches 1983

244	SGS 505W	Bedford YMT	1981 Duple Dominant II Express C53F

Ex Stephenson, Hullbridge 1983

201	A201 OKN	Bedford YNT	1983 Wright Contour C49F

Ex Shaw & Kilburn (dealer) 1984, to HKR 11 1984, to C53F 1985

202	B202 XKM	Bedford YNT	1984 Duple Laser C53F
206	JKX 726N	Bedford YMT	1974 Duple Dominant B53F

Ex Vauxhall Motors, Luton 1985

203	C203 GKR	Bedford YMT (automatic)	1986 Wright TT DP53F
288	Q288 JKO	Bedford YMT (automatic)	1986 Wright TT DP53F
205	C92 DTM	Scania K92	1985 Plaxton Paramount 3200 Mk2 C54F

Ex Scania UK, Milton Keynes 1986

214	BNO 701T	Bedford YMT	1979 Duple Dominant II Express C53F

Ex Metrobus, Orpington 1986

215	XPL 889T	Bedford YMT	1978 Duple Dominant B61F

Ex Metrobus, Orpington 1986

VEHICLES OUT OF FLEET:

1975: 998 AKT, 410/11 DKM, 413 GKT, 19 UKK.
1976: 414 GKT, 517 RKR, 20/2 UKK, 23 YKO.
1977: 412 DKM, 518 RKR, 21 UKK, EKP 233/4C, JKE 336/40-2E, AKE 147-50K, EKR 151-4L.
1978: 516 RKR, 24/5 YKO, EKP 227-32C, JKE 337/8E, OKJ 844F.
1979: JKE 335/9E, NKK 243F, OKM 145/6G.
1980: HKJ 255-8N, JKN 59-61N, HOR 335L.
1981: JKO 62-4N, HOR 334L, HNU 117/8/20/1N, SKN 491R..
1982: NKE 301-7P, GRC 883-5N, HNU 119/23N, JCH 398N, STD 119/21L, HKX 553V.
1983: HNU 126/4/5N, HKN 333V, MKP 336W.
1984: WKE 65S, WKM 70S.
1985: HNU 122N, WKE 67S, EKX 648T, AVS 903T, UKK 335X.
1986: AKK 171T, MKP 181W.
Remaining vehicles transferred to Boro'line Maidstone, 10/86.

Fleet No.	Reg No.	Chassis	Date Body
201	HKR 11	Bedford YNT	1983 Wright Contour C53F

To A35 SKL 1991.

202	B202 XKM%	Bedford YNT	1984 Duple Laser C53F

To 642 WKR 1989.

203	C203 GKR%	Bedford YMT (automatic)	1986 Wright TT DP53F
205	C92 DTM	Scania K92	1985 Plaxton Paramount 3200 Mk2 C54F

To 794 SKO 1988; C874 YKE 1991.

206	JKX 726N%	Bedford YMT	1974 Duple Dominant B53F
208-11	TKM 108-11X	Bedford YMT	1982 Wadham Stringer Vanguard B61F
214	BNO 701T%	Bedford YMT	1979 Duple Dominant II Express C53F
215	XPL 889T	Bedford YMT	1978 Duple Dominant B61F
226	26 YKO%	Leyland Titan PD2A/30	1963 Massey H33/28R

Carried No. 26.

232	CKN 332Y	Bedford YMQS (auto)	1982 Lex Maxeta B37F
237-41	CKM 137-41Y%	Bedford YMT	1982 Wright TT B61F
242-3	CKN 142-3Y%	Bedford YMT	1982 Wright TT DP53F
244	SGS 505W	Bedford YMT	1981 Duple Dominant II Express C53F
245	TER 5S%	Bedford YMT	1978 Duple Dominant II C53F
			Rebodied in 1989 Willowbrook Warrior B61F
260	ABH 760X%	Bedford YMQ (automatic)	1982 Wright TT B45F

To 851 PKJ 1991

266/7/9	WKE 66/7/9S	Bedford YMT (automatic)	1978 Duple Dominant B61F (269 %)
268	4066 KO	Bedford YMT (automatic)	1978 Duple Dominant B61F

To YKN 825S 1988.

272-6	AKK 172-6T	Bedford YMT (automatic)	1978 Duple Dominant B61F (272/5 %)

275 to 794 SKO 1991

277/8	JKJ 277/8V	Bedford YMT	1979 Duple Dominant II Express C53F
279-80	MKP 179-80W	Bedford YMT (automatic)	1981 Wadham Stringer Vanguard B61F
282/3	MKP 182/3W	Bedford YMT (automatic)	1981 Wadham Stringer Vanguard B61F
284/5	PKE 184/5W%	Bedford YMT	1981 Duple Dominant II Express C53F
288	Q288 JKO%	Bedford YMT (automatic)	1986 Wright TT DP53F

All ex Maidstone Borough Transport 1986.

259/62/3	GFN 559/62/0N	Bristol LHS6L	1975 Eastern Coach Works B35F

Ex East Kent, Canterbury 1986.

204	4066 KO%	Scania K92	1986 Plaxton Paramount 3500 Mk2 C55F
233-6	D233-6 MKK	Dodge S56	1986 East Lancs B25F
261	GFN 261N	Bristol LHS6L	1975 Eastern Coach Works B31F

Ex Kent Engineering, Canterbury 1986.

207	D207 MKK%	Scania K92CRB	1987 East Lancs B55F
212/3	D212/3 MKK%	Scania K92	1987 East Lancs H55/37F
227-9	D155-7 HML	Leyland Lynx LX112TL11RZ1	1987 Leyland B49F
216	562 PTU%	Bedford YMT	1981 Duple Dominant C42Ft

Ex Highfield, Wigan 1987.

219/22	A129/30 MBA	Leyland Tiger TRCTL11/3RZ	1983 Plaxton Paramount 3500 C49Ft
220/3	A126/3 MBA	Leyland Tiger TRCTL11/3RH	1983 Plaxton Paramount 3500 C48Ft
224	A124 MBA	Leyland Tiger TRCTL11/3RH	1983 Plaxton Paramount 3500 C49Ft

219/20/22-4 all ex Ribble, Preston 1987.

221	A776 JBG	Volvo B10M-61	1984 Duple Caribbean C48Ft

Ex Houghton, Liverpool 1987.

290	BUF 278C%	Leyland Titan PD3/4	1965 Northern Counties FH39/30F

Ex Thomas, Tonypandy 1987. To 217 UKL 1988. To BUF 278C 1992.

299	KEL 128	Leyland Titan PD2/3	1950 Weymann FH33/25D

Driver Training Bus.

Ex preservation 1988. To XKP 792A 1989. To KEL 128 1990

230/1	B334/48 AMH	Leyland Royal Tiger	1985 Van Hool Alizee C53F

Ex Travellers, Hounslow 1988. 230 to 851 PKJ 1989. B301 MKP 1991.

751-61	E151-61 OMD*	Leyland Olympian ON6LXB/1RH	1988 Optare H47/29F
764	E164 OMD*	Volvo Citybus B10MD	1988 Alexander RV H47/37F
701/2	E701/2 XKR*	Scania N112DRB	1988 Alexander RH H47/31F
246	PCW 511X%	Ford Transit	1982 Cheshire Conversions C12F

Ex Lancaster City Transport 1988.

251	F997 EKM%	MCW Metrorider MF159/2	1988 MCW B28F
252	F116 EKO%	MCW Metrorider MF159/2	1988 MCW B28F
253	F746 EKO%	MCW Metrorider MF159/2	1988 MCW B28F
254	F847 EKP%	MCW Metrorider MF159/2	1988 MCW B28F
286	A849 UYM	Leyland Royal Tiger	1984 Plaxton Paramount 3500 C49Ft

To KEL128 1989. A868 SKK 1990.

287	A853 UYM	Leyland Royal Tiger	1984 Plaxton Paramount 3500 C53F

286/7 both ex Cowie, London N16 1988.

901	THX 162S	Leyland-National 10351A	1978 B36D
902	AYR 345 T%	Leyland-National 10351A	1979 B36D
903/4	BYW 380/436V	Leyland-National 10351A	1979 B36D

901-4 all ex London Buses 1988

911	LES 48P%	Volvo Ailsa AB57	1976 Alexander H44/31D

Ex Tayside, Dundee 1988

912/3	NSP 313/4R	Volvo Ailsa AB57	1976 Alexander H44/31D

Ex Ensign, Purfleet 1988

914-8	NSP315/6/8/9/22R	Volvo Ailsa AB57	1976 Alexander H44/31D (914-6/8: %)

Ex Tayside, Dundee 1988/9

208/9	B48/6 DNY	Bedford YNT	1985 Duple Laser C53F

Ex Bebb, Llantwit Fadre 1988

980-3	D340/1/35/18 WPE*	Ford Transit	1986 Carlyle B16F

Ex Alder Valley, Aldershot 1989

762	F991UME*	Leyland Olympian ON6LXB/1RH	1988 Optare H47/29F

Entered service 1989. It was one of the three vehicles cancelled in 1988.

921-34	F101-14 TML*	Volvo Citybus B10M-50	1989 Alexander RV H47/29D
249	F241 JWV	MCW Metrorider MF154/13	1988 MCW B33F

Ex Chambers, Stevenage 1989. To 217 UKL 1992.

250	G298 SKP	MCW Metrorider MF154/2	1989 MCW C28F

To HKR 11 1991.

801-12	G34-45 VME*	Leyland Lynx LX2R11C15Z4S	1989 Leyland B49F
291/2	D122/3 HMT	Leyland Royal Tiger	1987 Van Hool Alizee C53F

Ex Travellers, Hounslow 1989

293-5	G970-2 KJX	DAF MB230LB615	1990 Van Hool Alizee H C51Ft
264	MOM 579P	Leyland Fleetline FE30AGR	1976 Park Royal H43/33F
265	KOM 315P	Leyland Fleetline FE30AGR	1976 MCW H43/33F
266/7	NOC 379/89R%	Leyland Fleetline FE30AGR	1976 MCW H43/33F

264-7 all ex West Midlands Travel 1990

296	E320 EVH%	DAF MB230LB625	1988 Van Hool Alizee H C51Ft

Ex Midland Scottish 1990

270/1	GVO 713/2N%	Leyland Atlantean AN68/1R	1975 East Lancs H47/31D
273/4	OTO 559/60M%	Leyland Atlantean AN68/1R	1974 East Lancs H47/31D

270-4 all ex City of Nottingham 1990

765-70	H765-770 EKJ*	Leyland Olympian ON2R50C13	1991 Northern Counties H47/30F
813-6	H813-6 EKJ*	Leyland Lynx LX2R11G15Z4S	1991 Leyland B49F
220-3	J995-8 GCP	DAF SB220LC550	1991 Ikarus B50F
210/1	OTO 541/6M%	Leyland Atlantean AN68/1R	1974 East Lancs H47/31D

Ex City of Nottingham 1991

297	E342 EVH%	DAF MB230LB615	1988 Duple 320 C53F

Ex Wood, Barnsley 1992

VEHICLES OUT OF FLEET:

1987: TKM 108 – 11X, JKJ 277V, MKP179/80/2/3W.

1988: CKN 332Y, A776 JBG.

1989: SGS 505W, AKK 173/4T, JKJ 278V, A126/32 MBA.

1990: WKE 66S, AKK 176T, GFN 560/2N, WKE 66S, A124 MBA, KEL 128, A124 MBA, KEL 128, A868 SKK (A849 UYM), A853 UYM.

1991: A35 SKL (A201 OKN), C874 YKE (C92 DTM), YKN 825S (WKE 68S), BNO 701T, XPL 889T, GFN 559/61N, A123/29 MBA, B301MKP (B334 AMH), B348 AMH, BYW 380V, NSP 313R, G970-2 KJX, MOM579P, KOM315P.

1992: D155-7 HML, THX 162S, BYW 436V, NSP314/9R, B46/8 DNY, 217 UKL (F241 JWV), HKR 11 (G298 SKP), J995-8 GCP.

*: To Kentish Bus 2/92.   %: Final fleet 5/92.

These four views of Wright bodied Bedford CKM 140Y were taken during its life in Maidstone. When nearly new in Douglas Road, Fant – to save money these vehicles had bulb lighting, which was only fitted on one side; in 1984 after the arrival of the 'three wise monkeys' advert and the smaller replacement windscreen; on 25 October 1986 at Downswood terminus with the cream area painted yellow ready for the start of Boro'line Maidstone the next day; finally in 1988 at Ashford in full Boro'line colours.